SUPER-
COMPLETELY
AND TOTALLY
THE
MESSIEST

SUPER- COMPLETELY AND TOTALLY THE MESSIEST

by Judith Viorst

illustrated by Robin Preiss Glasser

Atheneum Books for Young Readers

NEW YORK   LONDON   TORONTO   SYDNEY   SINGAPORE

Atheneum Books for Young Readers
An imprint of Simon & Schuster Children's Publishing Division
1230 Avenue of the Americas
New York, New York 10020
Text copyright © 2001 by Judith Viorst
Illustrations copyright © 2001 by Robin Preiss Glasser
Book design by Ann Bobco
The text of this book is set in Adobe Caslon.
The illustrations are rendered in pen and ink and watercolor.
Printed in Hong Kong
10 9 8 7 6 5 4 3 2 1
Library of Congress Cataloging-in-Publication Data
Viorst, Judith.
Super-completely and totally the messiest / Judith Viorst ; illustrated by Robin Preiss Glasser.
p. cm.
Summary: Olivia, who is very neat and practically perfect, despairs because her sister Sophie is
super-completely and totally the messiest person, no matter where she goes or what she does.
ISBN 0-689-82941-8 (alk. paper)
[1. Orderliness—Fiction. 2. Cleanliness—Fiction. 3. Sisters—Fiction.]
I. Preiss Glasser, Robin, ill. II. Title.
PZ7.V816 Sw 2000
[Fic]—dc21 00-021427

For my super-completely and totally terrific son Tony,
who gave me the neat idea for this messy book.
—J. V.

To my sister Lisa, far away, but close to my heart.
—R. P. G.

My room is very neat—like me, Olivia.

Jake, my big brother, is sort of, but not a HUGE slob.

And then there's my little sister, whose room is seriously—I mean seriously—REVOLTING. Which is one of maybe a MILLION reasons why my sister Sophie is super-completely and totally THE MESSIEST.

"Hello, is anyone home?" I ask, when I open the door to her room. Because even when she's there, it's hard to find her.

I mean, there's so much stuff on her bed that sometimes I just see the top of her head.

And there's so much stuff on her floor and spilling out of her dresser drawers that sometimes all I can find is a nose or a toe.

And there's so much stuff
in her closet that once when
she opened up her closet—

"Don't do it!" I hollered.
"Stop!
Watch out!
Oh no!"

— she super-completely and totally DISAPPEARED.

I mean, Sophie isn't just messy.
She is THE MESSIEST.

Maybe you think that Sophie isn't so messy when she's
in school. If you think THAT, you would be really wrong.

Maybe you think that she isn't a mess when she
puts on a fancy dress and goes to a birthday party.
If you think THAT, you would be REALLY wrong.

Maybe you even think that she could play with crayons or paints and not mess up ceilings and cats and herself and EVERYTHING. If you think THAT, you would be so really, REALLY wrong that it might be a year before you were right about ANYTHING.

I'm her big sister and some things I know for sure. And one thing I know for sure is that whatever Sophie does, she is THE MESSIEST.

Like, once we went
to the seashore, where
they were having a
sandcastle contest, and
Sophie was carrying just
her pail and her towel.

And just with her pail and her towel she super-completely and totally wrecked seven sandcastles.

And once we went to a circus where a juggler was juggling eggs and pitchers and flower pots. Sophie got to bring her kite along. And just by letting go of her kite Sophie wrecked the juggler, and a dozen eggs, and all of the pitchers and flower pots.

And once we went to a farm to visit some chickens and cows and a vegetable garden and pigs. Sophie's shoelaces were— they're ALWAYS—untied. All I can say is: Poor chickens. Poor cows. And poor, POOR vegetable garden.

No, I can say something else: I can say that all of the pigs on that farm thought that my sister Sophie was their cousin.

No, I'm NOT a rude person. I would never, ever, EVER call Sophie a pig. I'm only saying that PIGS think Sophie's a pig.

I'm only saying this: That wherever my sister Sophie goes, she is super-completely and totally THE MESSIEST.

I keep on telling Sophie, "Try to be neat, like me, Olivia." She says she'll try to be neat. But she forgets.

Our mom keeps telling Sophie, "Try to be careful, like Olivia." She says she'll try to be careful. But she forgets.

Our dad keeps telling Sophie, "Watch where you're going and watch what you're doing. Try to pay attention, like Olivia." She says she'll try to watch. She says she'll try to pay attention. But she forgets.

And so, when Sophie cleans up a mess it's a messier mess than it was before she started. When Sophie clears off the plates, they'll never, ever, EVER need to be cleared off again.

And if you bought a new car, and you gave Sophie a ride in that car, it would look like a really OLD car in about two minutes.

Sophie is ALWAYS making— and being—a mess.

Like last Halloween, when Sophie decided to wear a
nurse's costume. White hat. White uniform. White socks.
White shoes. She wanted to dress like a nurse because I
told her that a nurse is NEVER messy.

What I meant, of course, was a nurse isn't messy unless she's the sort of nurse who tricks and treats all over her white uniform.

Unless she's a nurse who gets candy corn stuck in her teeth.

Unless she's a nurse who FALLS IN when she bobs for apples.

Unless she's a nurse who could make you super-completely and totally sorry that you ever answered the doorbell on Halloween.

What I mean is, maybe you've met some messy people,
but you've never met anyone messier than Sophie.

Like, Sophie's got this hair—this frizzy, fuzzy, curly hair—
and it sticks out around her head like a cloud or a nest. And it
keeps getting bigger and higher, and bigger and higher, and
bigger and higher because she FREAKS if anyone tries to cut it.

Hey, Sophie, who's living in there—a couple of birds, a family of mice? That's what Jake sometimes says. He's only teasing.

But once when our dad was combing her hair he combed out a whistle, a ring, and a piece of a sandwich.

And once when our mom was combing her hair I thought I heard some chirping and some squeaks.

If you're looking to see messy hair—I mean, if you're looking to see messy ANYTHING—just look at Sophie.

I keep on telling Sophie, "Try to be more like me—Olivia."

She says she'll try to be me. But she forgets.

Our mom keeps telling Sophie, "Try to hold the plates tight, like Olivia." She says she'll try to hold tight.

But she forgets.

Our dad keeps telling Sophie, "Wipe off your mouth and your hands and your shoes. Try to be unchocolately, like Olivia." She says she'll try to wipe. She says she'll try to be unchocolately.

But she forgets.

And just listen to what happened when Sophie said to Jake and me
could we please help her make our mom breakfast in bed for Mother's Day.

No, she didn't spill the orange
juice. Jake and I helped her pour it.

She didn't burn the toast.
We helped watch the toast.

We also helped her to not smear the strawberry jam all over
the kitchen and to not put a TON of cereal in the bowl.

And our dad said he would make
coffee and bring it up later,
so Sophie didn't get to
mess up THAT.

Then all of us carefully
carried the tray to the bedroom.

Mom sat up in bed,
and we set down the tray.

Then Sophie felt so proud that she had made our mom breakfast in bed that she climbed on the bed and started yelling, "Yay! Yay!"

Except that while she
was yelling "Yay! Yay!"
she also jumped up and down,
which is NOT a good thing to do to breakfast in bed.
I mean, it was super-completely and totally UGLY.
I mean, NOBODY'S better at making a mess than Sophie.

Our mom says I should tell you that Sophie's a kind and very nice person, even though she messes up breakfasts and beds.

Our dad says I should tell you that Sophie's a smart and funny person, even though she wrecks sandcastles, jugglers, and vegetable gardens.

Jake says I should tell you that Sophie's great at puzzles and dancing, even though she's not great at cleaning her room.

Sophie says I should tell you that she didn't MEAN to drown the kitchen in water, even though she left the faucets running.

Sophie says I should tell you that she didn't MEAN to drown the kitchen in water, even though she left the faucets running.

And I would like to tell you that even though I would bet my best bracelet that Sophie will never be practically perfect, like me, I'm hoping that one of these days she'll start to remember to stop forgetting to try NOT to be so super-completely and totally THE MESSIEST.